Coyotes

by Grace Hansen

Abdo
ANIMALS OF
NORTH AMERICA
Kids

abdopublishing.com

Published by Abdo Kids, a division of ABDO, PO Box 398166, Minneapolis, Minnesota 55439.

Copyright © 2016 by Abdo Consulting Group, Inc. International copyrights reserved in all countries. No part of this book may be reproduced in any form without written permission from the publisher.

Printed in the United States of America, North Mankato, Minnesota.

102015

012016

THIS BOOK CONTAINS
RECYCLED MATERIALS

Photo Credits: iStock, Shutterstock

Production Contributors: Teddy Borth, Jennie Forsberg, Grace Hansen

Design Contributors: Laura Mitchell, Dorothy Toth

Library of Congress Control Number: 2015941774

Cataloging-in-Publication Data

Hansen, Grace.

 Coyotes / Grace Hansen.

   p. cm. -- (Animals of North America)

ISBN 978-1-68080-109-5 (lib. bdg.)

Includes index.

1. Coyote--Juvenile literature.   I. Title.

599.77/25--dc23

                    2015941774

Table of Contents

Coyotes

Coyotes live throughout North and Central America. They can be found in forests and prairies. They live in deserts and mountains, too.

5

Coyotes have big pointed ears. They have long tails.

Coyotes have fur. Their fur can be brown, tan, or gray. Their bellies are usually white.

9

Hunting & Food

Coyotes are fast. They have a strong sense of smell. They can see and hear well. These things make them great hunters.

Coyotes will eat many
things. Their favorite food
is rabbit. They also eat
fish, grass, and more.

13

Packs & Pups

Coyotes are social animals.
Most live together in groups
called packs. Each pack has
its own territory.

14

Mates dig burrows.

These burrows are

called **dens**. Mothers

and babies sleep in dens.

Baby coyotes are called pups. There are about 5 pups in each litter. Pups are very small when they are born. But they grow fast!

Pups learn to hunt by watching their parents. Some pups stay with their parents' pack. Other pups leave to start a new pack.

More Facts

- A coyote's tail can be 16 inches (40 cm) long.

- Most coyotes have yellowish eyes.

- Coyotes can run very fast. They can run up to 40 miles per hour (64 km/h).

Glossary

den – the home of some wild animals.

mates – a pair of animals that have offspring together.

social – an animal that lives with a group of its kind rather than alone.

territory – an area that an animal defends against others, especially of the same species.

Index

abdokids.com

Use this code to log on to abdokids.com and access crafts, games, videos, and more!

Abdo Kids Code:
ACK1095